Feathers and Flight

WELDON OWEN PTY LTD

Chairman: John Owen
Publisher: Sheena Coupe
Associate Publisher: Lynn Humphries
Managing Editor: Helen Bateman
Design Concept: Sue Rawkins
Senior Designer: Kylie Mulquin
Production Manager: Caroline Webber
Production Assistant: Kylie Lawson

Text: Robert Coupe
Consultant: George McKay, Conservation Biologist
U.S. Editors: Laura Cavaluzzo and Rebecca McEwen

04 03 02 01 00
10 9 8 7 6 5 4 3 2

Published in the United States by
Shortland Publications, Inc.
P.O. Box 6195
Denver, CO 80206-0195

Printed in Singapore
ISBN: 0-7699-0474-2

CONTENTS

A World of Birds

Wherever you live, you will see many different kinds of birds. Some birds always stay in one special kind of place, such as a desert or a rain forest. Others may fly across the oceans, or between countries that are far apart.

2

1

7

6

1. Ostrich
2. Falcon
3. Hummingbird
4. Albatross
5. Peacock
6. Rooster
7. Tawny frogmouth

BIRD MAPS

The colors on the maps show how many kinds of birds live in different parts of the world.

under 50 kinds		500–1,000 kinds
50–250 kinds		1,000–5,000 kinds
250–500 kinds		Over 5,000 kinds

BIRD BEGINNINGS

The world's first bird was the Archaeopteryx. It lived in the age of the dinosaurs, 150 million years ago. The pictures show what some other early birds looked like. Hesperornis lived about 100 million years ago. It did not fly and it ate fish. Teratornis was a hunter that lived in North America. Dinornis was a huge bird. It did not have wings, so it could not fly.

Hesperornis

Teratornis

6

STRANGE BUT TRUE

Archaeopteryx is the first bird we know about. Unlike today's birds, it had teeth.

Dinornis

BIG AND SMALL

A bee hummingbird is so small, it would fit in your hand. An ostrich is so tall, it stands higher than any human. In between are birds of every size. Some birds, like flamingos, have long legs for wading, and long necks for reaching down to catch fish. Others have wide, strong wings for flying long distances.

AMAZING!

Dodos lived on an island near Africa. Because they couldn't fly, they were easy to hunt. Now there are no more dodos.

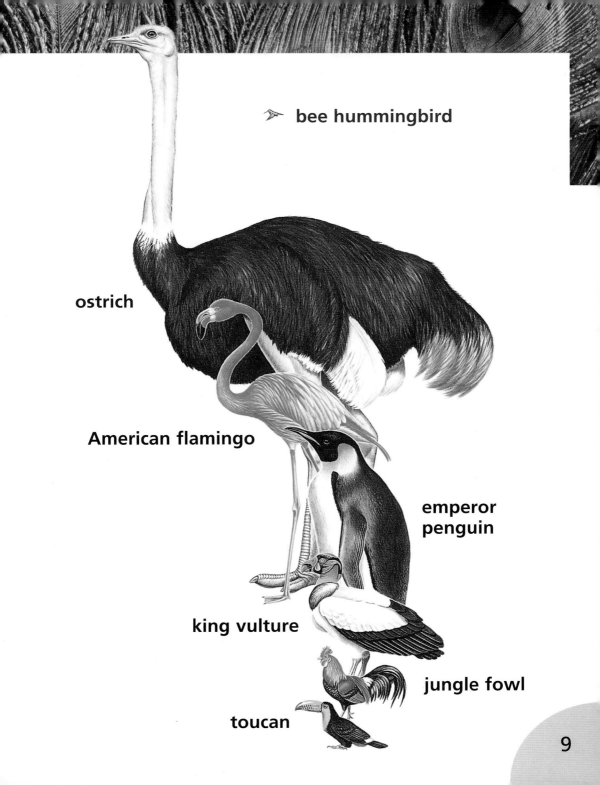

bee hummingbird

ostrich

American flamingo

emperor penguin

king vulture

jungle fowl

toucan

9

INSIDE OUT

It is easy to tell if an animal is a bird, because birds are the only animals that have feathers. Under these feathers, birds, like us, have skin. Inside are the

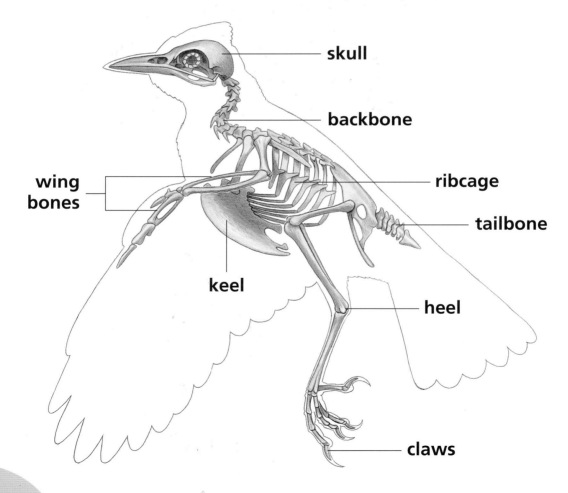

skull

backbone

wing bones

ribcage

tailbone

keel

heel

claws

bones that make up its skeleton. A bird's skeleton has a special shape that allows the bird to fly. Inside a bird's body are its heart, lungs, and other organs.

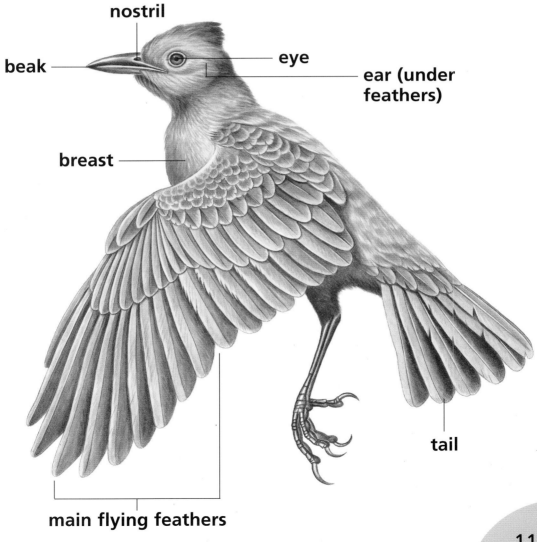

nostril

beak

eye

ear (under feathers)

breast

tail

main flying feathers

HOW DO BIRDS FLY?

Birds take off and fly through the air by flapping their wings. They have strong muscles in their chest that help them move the wings up and down. Most small birds keep their wings moving as they fly. Larger birds, such as eagles, can often glide on the wind, with their wings stretched out wide.

2. Tucking wings in

3. Spreading wings out

1. Taking off

HOVERERS

Hummingbirds hover in the air as they feed on flowers. While they hover, their wings spin around in circles.

wing muscles

4. Pushing forward

5. Finishing

BIRD BITS

Notice the differences between the birds on these pages. The king penguin and the brown pelican are water birds. Their webbed feet help them swim through the water, just as flippers help human swimmers. The California quail and the honey creeper are land birds. They have separate toes that let them walk easily on land.

King Penguin
This bird is built for swimming, but not for flying.

California Quail
This bird has an interesting topknot.

BEAKS AND BILLS

A bird's bill gives a clue to what it eats. The ground finch (top) eats seeds. The heron (bottom) reaches into water for fish. What kind of food do you think the eagle eats? Find out on page 29.

Brown Pelican
A skin sac under its big bill allows it to scoop up fish.

Honey Creeper
The long, thin bill of this bird can reach deep into flowers.

Eastern Rosella
This bird's long tail helps it keep its balance.

All birds have tails. Some have long tails and some have short tails. A tail helps a bird to keep its balance while it is flying and when it is on the ground or sitting on a branch. It is also like a rudder on a boat. It helps the bird change direction and to slow down while it is flying. Birds that do not fly often have short tails.

Puffin
This bird is a swimmer.

Blue-crowned Motmot
This bird uses the knobs at the end of its tail to attract other birds.

DID YOU KNOW?

A woodpecker hangs on to a tree trunk as it pecks at the bark. Its strong tail pushes against the tree and keeps the bird steady.

FEATHERS

Birds have three main kinds of feathers. The feathers underneath are called down feathers. They are small and soft and keep the bird warm. Contour feathers give the bird its shape and protect it from the weather. The flight feathers are in the wings and the tail. They are the feathers the bird uses to fly.

green-winged macaw

HOW FEATHERS GROW

A bird's feathers grow out of its skin. A new feather is like a tube. As it grows, the soft parts of the feather slowly unfold.

Owl
Its markings, or feather patterns, are easy to recognize.

contour feather

flight feather

down feather

mallard duck

19

RAINFOREST GLIDERS

flying gecko

flying frog

A few animals besides birds can
move through the air. But they do
not have wings and cannot fly a
long way. Some lizards, frogs,
possums, and squirrels are
members of this flying club. There is even one kind
of snake that can sail through the air. Most of these
animals live in the thick, damp forests that we call
rain forests. They all have flaps of skin that they
hold out like a parachute or a kite as they glide
from tree to tree.

flying dragon

DID YOU KNOW?

Flying squirrels and possums can glide further than most other gliders. Like birds, they use their tail to change direction.

PARADE OF PENGUINS

Penguins are divers, not fliers. They live in cool southern regions. It is easy to tell penguins from other birds, but it is harder to tell one penguin from another. As you can see, penguins are different in size, markings, and other ways, too. The largest penguin, the emperor penguin, grows about 3 feet (1 meter) tall. The smallest, the fairy penguin, is only a third as big.

emperor penguin

chinstrap penguin

yellow-eyed penguin

MAKE A PAPER PENGUIN

1 Fold a square of paper in half to make a crease. Unfold it.

2 Fold the bottom corner up.

3 Fold the paper in half again.

4 Fold the sides in. These are the wing flaps.

5 Fold the top down to make a crease. Then unfold it again.

6 Open the paper out and pull the tip forward.

7 Close the paper again and press the "head" flat.

Magellanic penguin

Fiordland penguin

fairy penguin

BIRDS OF PREY

Birds of prey hunt and eat other animals and birds. They have sharp hooked beaks, big round eyes, and strong claws. Most birds of prey are powerful fliers. Some of them swoop from high in the air to pick up living animals in their claws. Some feed mainly on the flesh of dead animals.

Andean Condor
This lives in South America. It belongs to the vulture family.

White-bellied Sea Eagle
This bird often robs other birds of their prey.

African Pygmy Falcon
This bird is only 8 inches
(20 centimeters) long.

Secretary Bird
This is the only member of
its family. It lives in Africa.
Look at its crest feathers
and its long, strong legs.

When you imagine a bird of prey, you probably think of an eagle or a vulture. These are large birds, with wide-stretching wings. Some birds of prey, though, are much smaller, and some are tiny. The smallest is only about 8 inches (20 centimeters) long from head to tail. It weighs just 8 ounces (35 grams).

Large and Small
This picture gives some idea of the sizes of different birds of prey. Compare them with the man at the bottom.

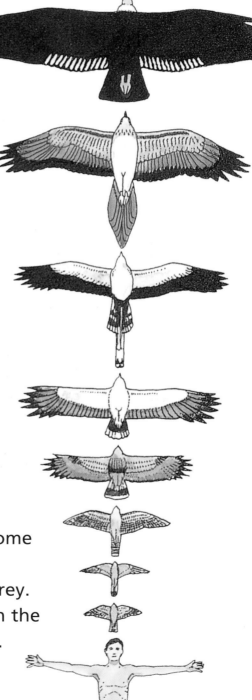

vulture

sparrowhawk

Did You Know?

Some birds of prey have long, thin toes and talons. Others have short, curved ones. Their feet and claws help them catch their food.

osprey

harpy eagle

27

Birds of prey all have large eyes and can see very clearly. An eagle, for example, can see more than twice as well as you can. It can spot its prey from far off, long before the animal knows that an eagle is near. Sometimes we say that people have an "eagle eye," meaning that they have very good sight.

EYES WITH TELESCOPES

The top rabbit picture shows how clearly a wedge-tailed eagle sees a rabbit from high in the air. The bottom picture shows how you would see it from the same place.

Bald Eagle
This North American
bird feeds mostly on
fish. But it will also
feed on any small
animal that it spots
with its "eagle eyes."

29

GLOSSARY

crest feathers Feathers that stand up on top of a bird's head.

gliders Animals, which are not birds, that can move through the air by using flaps of skin that they spread out wide.

markings The pattern of colors that a bird's feathers make.

prey Animals that are caught and eaten by other animals.

talons Sharp, curved claws that birds of prey have on their feet.

INDEX

CREDITS AND NOTES

Picture and Illustration Credits
[t=top, b=bottom, l=left, r=right, c=center, F=front, B=back, C=cover, bg=background]
Jocelyne Best 23tc. **Corel Corporation** 3r, 17rc, 18bl, 19tr, 30b. **Mike Gorman** 21br. **David Kirshner** 2t, 6bl, 6br, 7lc, 7tc, 8br, 10c, 11c, 12–13c, 14br, 14bl, 15bl, 15br, 15tc, 15rc, 16br, 16tr, 17tl, 21tc, 20tc, 22bl, 22bc, 22br, 23bl, 23bc, 23br, 29c, FCbl, FCtr, FCc, BC. **Frank Knight** 18br. **Graham Meadows Photography** 19bc, 19cl, 19c, 19cr. **Robert Morton** 4tc, 4bc, 4br, 4bl, 5tl, 5tc, 5bl. **Photodisc** 4–32 borders, Cbg. **Tony Pyrzakowski** 1c, 15tr, 24bl, 25br, 24br, 25tr, 26r, 27c, 28bc. **Trevor Ruth** 13tr, 31t. **Kevin Stead** 20rc. **David Wood** 4–5c, 5brc.

Acknowledgements
Weldon Owen would like to thank the following people for their assistance in the production of this book:
Jocelyne Best, Peta Gorman, Tracey Jackson, Andrew Kelly, Sarah Mattern, Emily Wood.